# The Redneck Joke Book

# The Redneck Joke Book

by

Jim Bob Buford
and
"Shotgun" Jack Grabowksi

**BARNES
&NOBLE
BOOKS**
NEW YORK

1997 Barnes & Noble Books

Design and typography by Noble Desktop Publishers

Cover cartoon by Jack Ziegler

ISBN 0-7607-0415-5  *casebound*
ISBN 0-7607-1529-7  *paperback*

Printed and bound in the United States of America

98 99 00 01 02 MC 9 8 7 6 5
99 00 01 02 03 MP 9 8 7 6 5 4 3 2 1

FG

*For all their help, we want to thank Ken Neill, Kevin Charlton, Helen Siskind Parsons, and others too numerous to mention.*

Randy took Maybelline to Birmingham to see a live play in a local theater. Unfortunately, all the seats were sold out.

"Sorry, but all we have left are two 'standing rooms'," explained the woman at the window.

"Only two left in 'standing room'?" said Randy. "Are they together?"

Bubba was bragging to the boys at the bar how ferocious his dog Spike was.

"My dog is the meanest dog in the world," he declared. "He's taken on pit bulls and Dobermans, and they're all afraid of him. No dog can lay a paw on Spike. I've got him tied up outside with a steel chain."

Just then, a mild-looking old man walked over to Bubba and spoke up, "I'm sorry, but I have to apologize to you. My dog just killed your Spike."

Bubba was flabbergasted. Beside himself with rage, he sputtered, "That's impossible! Your dog couldn't have killed Spike. What kind of a dog do you have?"

"He's a Chihuahua," the man meekly replied.

"What?" said Bubba incredulously. "How could your Chihuahua kill Spike?"

"He got stuck in his throat."

On his first trip to Nashville, Bobby Ray became friendly with the room clerk at his hotel. After talking together for a while, the clerk said, "I have a riddle for you. My father and mother had a baby. It wasn't my brother or sister. Who was it?"

Bobby Ray pondered the question for a while. "I give up," he finally said.

"It's me!" said the clerk.

When Bobby Ray got home, he rushed in to see his wife.

"I have a riddle for you," he told her. "My father and mother had a baby. It wasn't my brother or sister. Who was it?"

"I give up," said his wife. "Who was it?"

"A room clerk in Nashville!"

As somebody once observed, Southerners will be polite until they are angry enough to kill you.

*John Shelton Reed*

Boudreaux had just gotten cable TV for his house, and had settled down to watch a bullfight being broadcast from Mexico. He watched as each time the bull attacked, the matador pulled the cape aside and the bull barreled past him. Finally, unable to stand it any longer, Boudreaux yelled at the set, "You old fool, that bull ain't never gonna run into that sack unless you hold it still!"

Q. What do you call a redneck with half a brain?

A. Gifted.

In the middle of an especially hot Alabama day, Bryan collapsed in the middle of the street. A group of people quickly gathered around him, offering advice.

"Give him some air," said one man.

"Give him a shot of whiskey," offered a little old lady.

"Bring him to a hospital," commented another man.

"Raise his feet," yelled out another.

As one suggestion followed another, Bryan finally sat up and said, "Will all of you just keep quiet and listen to that sweet little old lady!"

Old man Perkins, the meanest man in town, finally died after a long illness. At the old man's funeral, the church was filled to overflowing with people.

"I don't believe this," said Dottsy. "I've never seen so many people here at one time."

"It just goes to show you," said Moose. "Give the people what they want and they'll come out."

Three rednecks were returning home from an evening of drinking beer at a roadside bar. All three were feeling no pain and their truck was weaving back and forth across the road. All of a sudden a police siren sounded and a squad car, with its lights flashing, roared up the road behind them. Stopping the truck, the driver said, "Quick! Everyone get in the back of the truck and get inside a potato sack. Maybe he'll think we've run off." So they jumped in the bed of their truck and each found a big potato sack to crawl into.

When the police officer walked up to the truck he shined his light on the first bag and tapped it. The first redneck warbled, "Meow."

"Wow," The officer whistled, "that's some cat."

When he got to the second bag, he tapped it with his foot. The redneck inside replied, "Woof!"

The officer thought, "Boy, that is some big dog."

Then he got to the third bag and tapped that.

A voice answered, "Potato."


Q. What do a tornado and a redneck divorce have in common?

A. Either way, someone's going to lose a trailer.


Two cows were standing in a field.

"Are you afraid of mad cow disease?" asked the first cow.

"Why should I be?" replied the other. "I'm a squirrel."


Three men were stranded on a deserted island: an Englishman, an Irishman, and a redneck. One day they discovered a magic lamp on the beach, and when they

rubbed it a genie appeared and gave them each one wish. The Irishman said that he really missed Dublin and he asked to be taken back to Ireland. In a moment he was gone.

Then it was the Englishman's turn and, following suit, he asked to be returned to London. Finally, it was the redneck's wish. When the genie asked him what he wanted, he looked around, "Well now that I'm all by myself, could you bring the other two guys back?"

Uncle Lester went to the police station to lodge a complaint.

"I've got three grown sons and we all live in one room. One of my sons has six cats, another has five dogs, the other has a goat."

"What's your problem?" the policeman asked.

"The smell is terrible. Can you do something about it?"

"Why don't you just open the window?" asked the policeman.

"What? And lose all my pigeons?"

I was in the backyard one beautiful day; I said to my mother, "Mama, why don't I have no brother and sister."

She said, "Go away and play. Don't worry your mother, dear. As lazy as your father was, you're lucky that you got here."

*Nipsy Russell*

*"This church is too poor to hire a minister of its own."*

Q. Do you know what a redneck's last words are?

A. Hey, fellas, watch this.

After eating dinner at a local diner, Clayton left the waitress three dimes as a tip. The next day, he came back again and got the same waitress. As he sat down, she said to him, "I can tell your fortune by the tip you left me yesterday."

"You can?" said Clayton. "Go ahead."

"Well," she began, "since the three dimes were left in a straight line, it shows you're very neat. The first dime shows that you're thrifty, and the second dime shows that you're a bachelor."

"Wow," marveled Clayton. "That's amazing. What does the third dime show?"

"The third dime shows that your father was a bachelor, too."


B.J. and Roy were discussing the mysteries of life over lunch.

"What would happen if you cut off one of your ears?" asked B.J.

"I guess I would lose some of my hearing," replied Roy.

"Then what would happen if you cut off both your ears?" continued B.J.

"I guess I'd go blind," answered Roy.

"What are you talkin' about?" asked B.J. "Why would you go blind if you cut off both your ears?"

"Because if I cut off both my ears, my hat would fall down over my eyes and I wouldn't be able to see."

ſing dinner at a local diner, Clayton left the three dimes as a tip. The next day, he came back again nd got the same waitress. As he sat down, she said to him, "I can tell your fortune by the tip you left me yesterday."

"You can?" said Clayton. "Go ahead."

"Well," she began, "since the three dimes were left in a straight line, it shows you're very neat. The first dime shows that you're thrifty, and the second dime shows that you're a bachelor."

"Wow," marveled Clayton. "That's amazing. What does the third dime show?"

"The third dime shows that your father was a bachelor, too."

B.J. and Roy were discussing the mysteries of life over lunch.

"What would happen if you cut off one of your ears?" asked B.J.

"I guess I would lose some of my hearing," replied Roy.

"Then what would happen if you cut off both your ears?" continued B.J.

"I guess I'd go blind," answered Roy.

"What are you talkin' about?" asked B.J. "Why would you go blind if you cut off both your ears?"

"Because if I cut off both my ears, my hat would fall down over my eyes and I wouldn't be able to see."

The diner was full of people when an earthquake hit the small North Carolina town.

"Don't worry," yelled one customer. "I'm from San Francisco. The best place to stand is in a doorway."

With that, everyone in the diner headed for the door, except for Connie, who was left standing in the middle of the room.

"What do I do?" she wailed. "I'm from Durham."

Buddy walked in his door one evening and said to his wife, "I just had the worst day ever. I started driving home and all of a sudden I hear, 'thump, thump, thump'—a flat tire. I pulled the truck over, changed the tire, and started up again. Would you believe it? Again I start hearin' 'thump, thump, thump'."

"That's terrible," said his wife. "What are the odds of that happening—A second flat tire?"

"Actually it wasn't," explained Buddy. "The first time I changed the wrong one."

Q. How can you keep a redneck busy for a month?

A. Give him a bag of M&Ms and ask him to alphabetize them.

Two successful businessmen, sitting next to each other on a flight to Knoxville, were talking about their sons' college plans.

"Mine is trying to decide between Alabama and Vanderbilt," said the first.

"Oh, don't let him go to Alabama," said the second. "They only have two kinds of students there: football players and women who are uglier than alligators."

"I'll have you know my wife went to Alabama," yelled the first man, jumping out of his seat.

"Really?" said the second, thinking quickly. "What position did she play?"

My Aunt Velveeta lets that stupid dog of hers sit right next to her in the dining room. And when she gets done eating, she will take her plate and let that dog lick it clean right at the table! Then she'll put some Poli-Grip on it and slip it right back in her mouth.

*Heywood Banks*

Dillard got a call from his doctor who said, "I've got some good news for you and some bad news."

"Oh, no," gasped Dillard. "Tell me the good news first, Doc."

"I'm afraid you have an incurable disease," said the doctor. "You'll be dead within twenty-four hours."

"What?" shouted Dillard. "If that's the good news, what's the bad news?"

"Well, I tried calling you yesterday, but you were out fishing."

George applied for a job as a bouncer in a bar. Looking over his application, the manager observed, "I see here that you've been fired from every job you've ever had."

"Yup," said George proudly. "I ain't no quitter."

Ray came home one night to find his house on fire. He rushed next door and called the fire department.

"Come quick," he yelled. "My house is on fire!"

"Okay," responded the chief. "How do we get there?"

"Don't you still have those big red trucks?"

Q. How many rednecks does it take to eat a possum?

A. Three. One to eat it and two to watch for cars.

A man walked into a store and the clerk asked him if he could be of any help.

"Yes," the man replied. "Do you have any country sausage?"

"Are you a redneck?" asked the clerk.

"What kind of question is that?" demanded the man. "If a man comes in and asks for Polish sausage, do you ask him if he's a Pollack? If someone asks for Italian sausage, do you ask him if he's a Dago? If a woman asks you for Bratwurst, do you ask her if she's a Kraut?"

The clerk shook his head. "No, but this is a hardware store."


Whipple's big-city cousin arrived at the farm for a vacation just in time to find Whipple helping a cow who was giving birth. As the calf emerged from the cow, his cousin's eyes got bigger and bigger. Finally he said, "Say, do you have any idea how fast that little cow was going when it ran into the big one?"


Dorsey and his wife, Betty Sue, had an argument which left Betty Sue in tears.

"This is how you treat me after I gave you the best years of my life," she bawled.

"If them were the best years," replied Dorsey, "I'm glad I didn't have to spend the other ones with you."


I grew up on a big farm. Last time I was home visiting my folks I delivered a calf. I tell ya, I feel so much thinner now.

*Henriette Mantel*

Bobby was out duck hunting when he was approached by the game warden, who asked to see his license.

The warden looked at the license and handed it back. "You can't hunt here with that," he said. "This is last year's license."

"That's okay," Bobby replied. "I'm only shooting at ducks I missed last year."

Q. What advice do redneck mothers give their children?

A. Never take candy from a stranger, unless he offers you a ride.

Aunt Patsy went to the sheriff to tell him Uncle Joe was missing.

"Can you give me a description of him?" asked the sheriff.

"He's short and bald and skinny and wrinkled and wears false teeth," answered Aunt Patsy. "Come to think of it, most of him was missing before he was."

A tourist came to a fork in the road and stopped. Spotting a boy by the road, he yelled out, "Hey, kid, does it matter which road I take to Tuscaloosa?"

"Not to me it don't," replied the boy.

*"Pooh white trash."*

The two preachers were having dinner together and Jones was telling Smith about a small problem he had at his church: His umbrella was missing and he believed one of the parishioners took it.

"I think I know how to find out who took it," said Jones. "On Sunday, I'm gonna give a sermon on the Ten Commandments. When I get to the one about 'Thou shalt not steal,' I'm gonna stare real hard at every person in church. The culprit will get all embarrassed and return it."

The next week, the two men got together again, and Smith asked how his plan worked.

"It would have worked fine," said Jones, "except that when I got to the part about 'Thou shalt not commit adultery,' I remembered where I left it."

Uncle Carl had been drinking moonshine for so many years, his body shook all over.

"You must drink an awful lot," observed his neighbor Mrs. Perkins.

"Nope," said Carl. "I spill most of it."

A medical supply salesman was passing through a small Kentucky town during one extremely hot August afternoon, and dropped by the local doctor's office.

"How's the doctor standing the heat?" he asked the nurse.

"Don't really know," she replied. "He's only been dead three days."

Hampton went to the neighborhood barber for a haircut.

"How does it look?" asked the barber when he was finished.

"Just about perfect," said Hampton, "but could you make it just a little longer in the back?"

Billy, Henson, and Betty Sue were out walking near the farm one day when a bird flew over them and dropped a messy deposit on Billy's head. Betty Sue looked on in disgust, then said, "Don't worry, Billy, I'll run back inside and get some toilet paper."

As she ran back toward the house, Billy turned to Henson. Pointing to his head he said, "You know, that Betty Sue ain't got much up here. That bird'll be miles away by the time she gets back."

Q. How do you break a redneck's finger?

A. Hit him in the nose.

"Archie," said Doc Jones, "you look worse than ever! When you came in last time, I told you to drink warm water an hour before each meal. Have you been doing it?"

"Well, no," answered Archie. "I been trying to, Doc, but I can only keep it up for about fifteen minutes."

It was so hot I seen a cow lying on her back giving herself a shower.

*Homer Haynes*

Preacher Perkins was in the middle of his sermon on Sunday when he yelled out, "Anybody who likes sin, stand up!"

Nobody in church stood except Uncle Robert.

"What are you doing, Robert?" exclaimed the preacher. "Do you mean to tell me you can stand up here in church and admit you like sin?"

"Excuse me, preacher," said Uncle Robert, sitting down sheepishly. "I thought you said gin."

Some Virginia good ole boys got together for their annual fox hunt and, without thinking, Merle brought along his female dog Lass to be part of the pack. Unfortunately, Lass was in heat. As soon as the hunt began, the dogs took off as fast as could be, with the hunters trying to keep up with them. Soon the pack had disappeared. The hunters arrived at old man Hank's place, where they spotted him sitting on his porch.

"Have you seen a bunch of dogs and a fox go by here, Hank?" asked one of the hunters.

"Yup," answered Hank. "And you know, it was the dangdest thing. That's the first fox hunt I ever did see where the fox was running fifth."

Q. What is XXX?

A. Three rednecks co-signing a note.

Brenda Lee was talking to Sally about a problem she had.

"A skunk got into our basement last week and the smell is driving us crazy," she said. "You got any ideas about how to get rid of him?"

After thinking it over for a few seconds, Sally replied, "Sure. Leave a trail of bread crumbs from the basement into the woods. The skunk'll eat the bread crumbs and follow the trail right out of the house."

Later that day, the two met up again.

"How'd it go?" asked Sally.

"Thanks for nothin'," snarled Brenda Lee. "Now we got *two* skunks in the basement!"


Preacher Pitts was lecturing young Connie about sin.

"Do you know where little boys and girls go when they do bad things?" asked the preacher.

"Sure," answered Connie. "Behind Moose's barn."


Maynard and his neighbor were talking.

"How you been feeling lately?" asked the neighbor.

"Oh, I been kind of sickly," replied Maynard. "Doc Jones gave me some pills to take every day with a little corn whiskey."

"Are you feelin' any better now?"

"Not too bad, considerin' I'm two weeks behind on the pills and five weeks ahead on the whiskey."

After living all their lives with an outhouse, Pearl and Johnny finally joined the modern age and got indoor plumbing. Anxious to try it out, Pearl sat down on the seat before the varnish was dry and became stuck. Try as he might, Johnny could not loosen her from the seat. Finally he gave up, unscrewed the seat from the toilet, and brought Pearl to the emergency room at the hospital.

Embarrassed, Pearl said to the doctor, "I bet you never seen nothing like this before."

"Sure I have," replied the doctor. "But I've got to admit, this is the first time I've ever seen one framed."

"My wooden leg was hurtin' me something fierce last night," complained Rob to his neighbor.

"That's impossible," said the neighbor. "How can a wooden leg hurt you?"

"My old lady hit me over the head with it," replied Rob.

The teacher called Crystal's mother to come to school.

"I asked Crystal who signed the Declaration of Independence," she explained, "and she said, 'Damned if I know.' I think you ought to do something about this."

Crystal's mother grabbed the girl by the hair.

"If you signed the damn thing, admit it!" she yelled.

Two farmers were boasting about the strongest kind of wind they'd seen.

"Out here in California," said one, "I've seen the fiercest wind in my life. You know those giant redwood trees? Well, the wind got so strong, it bent them right down."

"That's nothing," said the other. "Back on my farm in Iowa, we had a terrible wind one day that blew a hundred miles an hour. It was so bad one of my hens had her back turned to the wind and she laid the same egg six times."

*Joe Laurie, Jr.*

Beauford, Till, and Rowdy were sitting around lighting matches. Beauford struck the first one, but it didn't work so he threw it away. Till did the same with the second. When the third one lights up, Rowdy quickly blew it out, saying, "This one works! I'm gonna save it for later."

A good ole boy is somebody that rides around in a pickup truck and drinks beer and puts 'em in a litter bag. A redneck rides around in a pickup truck and drinks beer and throws 'em out the window.

*Billy Carter*

Q. What do you call duct tape in Kentucky?

A. Chrome.

# DID YOU HEAR ABOUT...

. . . the redneck who wondered if he divorced his wife would she still be his sister?

. . . the redneck who took a book out of the library called *How to Hug*? It turned out it was volume 10 of the encyclopedia.

. . . the redneck track star who won a gold medal in the Olympics? He was so proud of it, he went and got it bronzed.

. . . the redneck girl who canceled her wedding because she heard her friends were going to give her a shower?

. . . the redneck hemophiliac who tried to cure himself with acupuncture?

. . . the redneck housewife who couldn't double a recipe, because her oven wouldn't go up to 700 degrees?

"I saw a big buck deer last week, and I took two quick shots."

"What happened?"

"Nothing. By the time I got the cork back on the jug, he was gone."

Elvira stopped at her fence to talk to a neighboring farmer, who was driving by in his truck.

"What you got in your truck?" asked Elvira.

"Oh, I got a load of manure to put on my strawberries," replied the farmer.

"Well, everyone to their own taste," nodded Elvira. "I prefer cream and sugar on mine."

Roy and Wanda were reminiscing about their marriage.

"I think I been pretty good to you," said Roy. "When we got married, I told you I'd carry you over all the rough places in life."

"That's right," replied Wanda. "And you ain't missed a single one of them, either."

Roscoe and Red were in the yard when a rooster ran by chasing after a hen. Roscoe took some corn out and tossed it at the rooster, who stopped in his tracks and started eating the corn.

"I sure hope I never get that hungry," observed Red.

Cousin Bart, down from Atlanta, was visiting Bobby and his family. Since the house was so small, Bart and Bobby had to share a bed. The first night, Bart observed Bobby kneeling by the side of the bed. Thinking he should do the same to show that he was brought up right, Bart knelt on the other side of the bed to say his prayers.

"Boy, you're sure gonna be in trouble," said Bobby. "The pot's on this side of the bed."

You think I don't have culture just because I'm from Georgia. Believe me, we got culture here. We've always had sushi. We just used to call it bait.

*Congressman Ben Jones*

Tracy was working at the local fast food restaurant when a man came in to place an order.

"I'll take two hamburgers," he said, "one with onions and one without."

"Okay," said Tracy brightly. "Which one do you want without the onions?"

"Did you hear about Thelma?" asked Aunt Brenda. "She just had triplets. Doc Jones said that happens only once every 200,000 times."

"Wow," said Ellie May. "How does she ever find time to do the housework?"

Uncle Del hired himself out on weekends as a guide for duck hunters. Taking a group out one Saturday, they found themselves completely lost.

"I thought you said you were the best guide in Arkansas," yelled one of the hunters. "How come we're lost?"

"That's true," replied Uncle Del, "but I think we're in Tennessee now."

Ellie May had a reputation for her fun-loving ways, and Reverend Johnson was getting worried about her. Meeting her at the store, the Reverend stopped and said solemnly, "Ellie May, I prayed for you three times last night."

"That wasn't necessary," said Ellie May. "All you had to do was call and I would have come right over."

Chitlins? That pig's intestines! That includes the lower tract. Ain't no food down in that area. Chitlins—I think somebody misspelled that word.

*Bill Cosby*

Chip was complaining to Elvis about the vet, Doc Jones.

"I couldn't get my mule to take the pill he was supposed to have," said Chip, "so Doc Jones told me to put the pill in a tube and blow it straight down the mule's throat."

"Sounds like a good idea to me," said Elvis.

"Not if the mule blows first."

When unexpected company arrived for supper, Aunt Betty had to think of something to make the food last. She gathered all the kids together and said to them, "I don't have enough food to go around, so when I ask who wants hog jowls, I want you all to say, 'No thanks, I don't want any.'"

Supper proceeded as planned. By dessert time, all the kids who didn't have the hog jowls were really hungry, and couldn't wait to have some of the pie.

"All right," said Aunt Betty, "now everybody who didn't eat their hog jowls—no pie!"

Whitey and Rick were watching a John Wayne movie on television. Just as the cowboy jumped on his horse to ride away, Whitey turned to Rick and said, "I'll bet you ten dollars that his horse steps in a hole and he falls off."

"You're on," said Rick.

Sure enough, the horse proceeded to step in a hole, and John Wayne fell to the ground. Rick grumbled but paid Whitey the ten dollars. A bit embarrassed, Whitey admitted to Rick, "You know, I saw this movie before. That's why I knew he would step in the hole."

"I saw it, too," replied Rick, "but I never thought the horse'd be dumb enough to step in the same hole twice."

"My hobbies are huntin' and drinkin'," said Rufus.

"What do you hunt?" asked Jeb.

"Somethin' to drink," replied Rufus.

Q. When the mugging victim was brought into the room, what did the redneck in the police lineup say?

A. "Yup, that's her all right."

Little Betty Sue came home from school all agitated.

"We sure had some excitement at school today," she said.

"What happened?" asked Mama.

"Well, a little mouse got into our room and ran right up Miss Haversham's leg. She reached down, put her arms around her skirt, and squeezed. She must have squeezed a whole quart of water out of that poor little mouse!"

Uncle Beasley, with fire in his eyes, lined up all his kids.

"Which one of you pushed over the outhouse?" he demanded.

Carleen, thinking honesty would count in her favor, said, "I cannot tell a lie, Uncle Beasley, I did it."

With that, Uncle Beasley proceeded to give her a good whipping.

"That's not fair," sobbed Carleen. "When George Washington chopped down the cherry tree and told the truth, his pa didn't whip him."

"That's right," said Uncle Beasley, "but his pa wasn't in the cherry tree at the time!"

Q. Where did the redneck find a turtle with no legs?

A. Right where he left it.

Preacher Smith paid a visit to the Webster farm. While he was there, he noticed targets everywhere he looked—on the barn, on trees, on the well, on the scarecrow. Incredibly, each one of the targets had a bullet hole right in the center.

"Wow," said the preacher. "Who's the marksman around here?"

"I am," said nine-year-old Luke Webster.

"That's amazing," gushed Preacher Smith. "How can anyone be so perfect?"

"Oh, it's easy," answered Luke. "I just shoot first, then draw all the circles around the holes later."


For weeks someone had been coming around at night stealing watermelons from the Hargus farm. Mr. Hargus tried putting up signs that read DO NOT ENTER; NO TRESPASSING; and KEEP OUT, but all to no avail. Finally, he asked his neighbor for advice. The neighbor suggested that he post a new sign and Hargus followed his advice. The sign read: BEWARE! ONE OF THESE WATERMELONS HAS BEEN POISONED WITH CYANIDE!

The next day the two met again.

"How did my suggestion go?" asked the neighbor.

"Not too well," sighed Hargus. "I put up the sign last night like you said, but by this morning someone changed the wording. Look over there," he said, pointing at the sign: BEWARE! NOW *TWO* OF THESE WATERMELONS HAVE BEEN POISONED WITH CYANIDE!

Ken and Freddie were out on the lake fishing one beautiful Sunday morning when the church bells started ringing out in the distance. Ken looked over his shoulder at Freddie and said, "Don't you feel kind of guilty being out here fishing when church is about to start?"

"Not really," said Freddie. "I couldn't have gone to church today, anyway."

"Why not?" asked Ken.

"The wife's sick."

While out on a camping trip, Junior was just getting ready to eat. A pot of coffee was boiling, and a pan of bacon was frying on the fire. Just then, Junior heard a loud noise coming his way through the trees. All of a sudden, he saw an enraged black bear charging toward him. Riding the bear was the meanest looking man he'd ever seen, whipping the animal with a five-foot long rattlesnake. As they stampeded toward the campsite, the man yelled, "Whoa!" and the bear came to a skidding halt. The man jumped down off the bear, turned and punched the animal right between the eyes, knocking him out cold. He then picked up the rattlesnake, bit its head off, and tossed it into the nearby creek. Next, he reached for the pot of coffee and drank the boiling liquid right down. He grabbed the bacon with his bare hand, gobbled it up, then washed it down with the scalding hot grease from the pan. He wiped his face with a clump of poison ivy, grabbed some cold water and tossed it in the bear's face to revive him. He then picked up another rattlesnake, jumped back on the bear's back, and began to ride away. Looking back over his shoulder, he yelled to Junior, "Thanks a lot for the food, friend. I hate to eat and run, but there's a real baaaaaaaaad son-of-a-gun chasin' after me."

C.J. was given an oak bucket by his mother and sent to get some drinking water from the creek. Five minutes later, he came running back as if he's seen a ghost, with the empty bucket in his hand.

"What's the matter, C.J.?" asked his mother.

"I was just about to get some water," gasped C.J., "when I looked up and saw this five-foot long alligator in the water, just layin' there lookin' at me."

"Now, now," said his mother, "there's no need to be upset. Just remember, that alligator is probably more afraid of you than you are of it."

"If that's true," said C.J., "there's no point in me going back, 'cause that water ain't fit for drinkin'."

Jerry Jeff was visiting Washington state on his vacation when he came upon a farmer in an apple orchard.

"How much are your apples?" asked Jerry Jeff.

"All you can pick for a dollar," replied the farmer.

"Okay," said Jerry Jeff. "Give me two dollars worth."

Homer was reading a letter to Ray just as Bob came by.

"What are you doin'?" asked Bob.

"Ray just got a letter from his girlfriend, but he can't read, so I'm reading it to him," explained Homer.

"But how come you got cotton in your ears?" asked Bob.

"He don't want me to hear what she has to say."


While on a trip to New York City, Hollis was jumped by a couple of muggers. He put up a tremendous fight, but eventually the muggers pinned him to the ground and searched his pockets. But all they were rewarded with was seventy-five cents in change.

"Do you mean to tell me you put up such a fight just to save seventy-five cents?" shouted the first mugger.

"Heck, no," said Hollis. "I thought you were after the thousand dollars I keep in my shoe."


Clyde and Thomas were talking about the other farmhands where they work.

"I hear the boys are going out on strike," said Clyde.

"What for?" asked Thomas.

"Shorter hours," replied Clyde.

"That's great," agreed Thomas. "I always thought sixty was too many minutes for an hour."

*"Your prayers have been answered. I'm the DNA fairy."*

The diner at the local truck stop was furious.

"My steak is too rare," he shouted, but Hattie the waitress ignored him. He shouted again. "Didn't you hear me say, 'well done'?"

"I sure did," Hattie yelled back, "and I can't thank you enough. I hardly ever get any compliments."

The NRA is attempting to lift the ban on machine-gun sales. Well, as an avid hunting enthusiast, I've been hoping to buy a fully automatic Uzi in time for the duck-hunting season. One thing about a machine gun, it really takes the guesswork out of duck hunting.

*Mark Russell*

The census taker found Uncle Jack's shack and knocked on his door. When Jack asked what he wanted, the census taker replied, "The President sent us across the country to find out how many people live in the United States."

"Sorry you came all the way out here," said Uncle Jack. "I haven't the faintest idea."

New bride Carleen was talking with her cousin, Thelma Lou.

"I have my husband eating out of my hand," bragged Carleen.

"Sure does beat washing dishes, don't it?" replied Thelma Lou.

Since she was laid up with the flu and couldn't leave the house, Aunt Jennie sent Uncle Bob to the department store to buy her a new corset. He went to the lady's department, and explained the situation to the saleswoman.

"Certainly we can help you," she said. "Bust?"

"Nope," replied Uncle Bob. "I think it just plain wore out."

Linford planned on spending the week clearing some trees from his land, so he went to the hardware store to buy a new saw. The clerk took the opportunity to sell him a new chain saw, which he said would allow Linford to cut three or four cords of wood a day. Linford quickly bought the chain saw.

The next day, Linford worked eight hours but only managed to cut one cord of wood. The following day, he got up earlier, but still only managed to cut one cord. The third day, he worked right through lunch and supper, but only managed to cut one and a half cords of wood. The next day, Linford brought the saw back to the store, complaining that something must be wrong.

"Okay," said the clerk taking the chain saw. "Let's see what's the matter."

With that, he pulled the cable and the chain saw started up with a roar.

"Damn!" said Linford, leaping back with a start. "What's that noise?"

After Momma gave birth to twelve of us kids, we put her up on a pedestal. It was mostly to keep Daddy away from her.

*Dolly Parton*

Thomas had a wonderful bird dog that finally died of old age, so he was in the market for a new one. An old farmer raved about a dog he had available, and Thomas was interested. But before he put down his money, he insisted on a demonstration. The farmer agreed, so the two men and the dog went for a walk. After about five minutes, the dog stopped and pointed toward a clump of bushes, then rolled over two times.

"That means there are two birds in the bush," whispered the farmer. Sure enough, two birds soon flew out of the clump of bushes.

A little while later, the dog again stopped short. He pointed toward another bush, and proceeded to roll over on the ground five times.

"That means there are five birds in that bush," said the farmer. Almost immediately, five birds flew out of the clump.

The men continued walking until the dog again stopped. This time he began jumping up and down and running in circles. Next, the dog picked up a branch in his paw, started waving it violently, then dropped it at the two mens' feet.

"What in the world is he trying to tell us?" asked Thomas.

"Impressive," said the farmer. "That means there are more birds in that bush than you can shake a stick at."

Bryan and Linda May got married, and Bryan built a log cabin for the couple to live in. In a tree near the cabin he hung a large bell which had a rope attached to it.

"If you ever need me when I'm working in the field," explained Bryan to his wife, "all you have to do is ring the bell and I'll hear you and come running. But only ring it for emergencies."

The next day he was out in the field when he heard the bell. He rushed back to the cabin to find his wife at the front door. "I thought you might like a snack before lunch," she said.

Annoyed, Bryan said to her, "I told you that the bell should only be rung for emergencies!"

That afternoon, the bell rang again. Bryan raced home to be met by Linda May, who said, "The sink in the kitchen is backed up."

Furious, Bryan repeated, "The bell should only be rung for emergencies!"

Late that afternoon, the bell rang yet again. Upon arriving home, Bryan found the cabin in flames, the barn burned to the ground, and all his cattle fleeing down the road.

"Now," said Bryan, "that's more like it!"


Q. What's the difference between a rich redneck and a poor redneck?

A. Whitewalls on their wheelbarrows.

Preston was describing his childhood to Joe.

"My daddy's farm had two hundred cows," he said. "My two brothers and me had to divvy up the milking every day."

"That was some job for three boys," said Joe.

"Yup," Preston went on. "And it plumb drove us crazy until Daddy bought a hundred more cows."

"How did buying a hundred more cows help?" asked Joe.

"Well," answered Preston, "any fool can divide *three hundred* by three."

On the first day of fall, cousin Sally brought her six little ones to the new school. She introduced herself to the principal, who asked her how old her children were.

"The two youngest are six, the next two are eight, and the oldest two are ten," she said.

"That's amazing," exclaimed the principal. "Do you get two every time?"

"Shucks, no," replied Sally. "Sometimes we don't get any."

One of Uncle Jeb's farmhands went to Doc Adams to get his broken leg fixed up. The doctor took one look at it and asked him how it happened.

"Well," he began, "twenty-five years ago, when I first started working here, Jeb's daughter Ellie May came up to my room after supper one night. She had on this low-cut

dress, and was carrying me a piece of pie for dessert. When I finished it, she asked me if there was anything else I wanted and I told her 'No.' She said, 'Are you sure?' and I told her 'No, thanks.' She leaned over my chair and whispered in my ear, 'Are you really sure? Isn't there *anything* I can do for you?' 'No,' I repeated, 'I'm sure.'"

"That's an interesting story," said Doc Adams, "but what does that have to do with your broken leg?"

"This morning, when it dawned on me what she meant, I fell off the roof!"

The clerk at the desk of the New York City hotel answered a frantic call from Beau in Room 1034.

"You gotta help me," yelled Beau. "I'm trapped here in my room!"

"What do you mean you're trapped in your room?" asked the clerk.

"There are three doors in here," explained Beau. "One goes to the closet, one goes to the bathroom, and the third one has a sign on it saying, 'Do Not Disturb'!"

Judd's wife had been acting strangely, so he brought her to a psychiatrist.

"For the last six months," he explained, "she thought she was a lawnmower."

"Six months?" replied the psychiatrist. "Why have you waited so long to bring her in?"

"Well," answered Judd, "I had to wait for Linton to return her."

The new bride was complaining about her husband to her neighbor.

"When we got married," she said, "he told me he'd love me till the cows come home. How was I to know he was a cattle rancher?"

Tom and Sue were celebrating their fiftieth wedding anniversary and their kids threw them a big party. During the celebration, Sue noticed a tear coming out of Tom's eye.

"Oh, Tom," she said. "I never knew how sentimental you could be."

"That's not it," replied Tom. "You remember when your father caught us in the barn and said if I didn't marry you, he'd send me to jail for fifty years? Well, today I would have been a free man!"

A group of rednecks who were deer hunting decided to pair off in twos. A couple of hours later, Billy Ray was seen coming back to the cars carrying an eight-point buck on his shoulders.

"Where's Jethro?" asked one of the others.

"He fainted a while back there on the trail," was Billy Ray's reply.

"You mean you left him back there by himself and carried the deer?" asked another.

"I gotta admit, it was a tough call," said Billy Ray. "But then I figured, no one is gonna steal Jethro."

Q. Why were the rednecks pushing their house down the road in the middle of winter?

A. They were trying to jump-start the furnace.

A car traveling along a lonely country road sputtered to a halt. The driver got out to look under the hood, when he looked up to see a cow looking over his shoulder.

"I think it's your radiator," said the cow.

The shocked motorist jumped back and began running to a nearby farmhouse. He knocked on the door and the farmer answered.

"A cow outside just gave me advice about my car!" sputtered the motorist.

"Did the cow have big black spots?" asked the farmer.

"Why, yes," replied the motorist.

"Oh, don't listen to her," said the farmer. "She doesn't know anything about cars."

Eb and Keith were out hunting when they suddenly realized they were lost.

"What'll we do?" asked Eb.

"Don't worry," replied Keith. "All we have to do is shoot into the air three times, stay right where we are, and someone will come and find us."

So Eb fired into the air three times, but an hour passed and they were still alone. They decided to try it again, so Eb fired three more times into the air, and again they waited. Another hour passed and still no one arrived to find them.

"Let's try it one more time," said Keith.

"Alright," said Eb. "But it better work this time. We're down to our last three arrows."

Uncle Tike's barn burned to the ground, so Aunt Ellie got on the phone to the insurance company.

"Our barn burned down," she explained. "We'd appreciate it if you'd send us our check for fifty thousand dollars, the amount of our insurance."

"I'm sorry," replied the man from the company. "We don't give money out. We replace the barn and all the equipment in it."

"In that case," said Aunt Ellie, "cancel the policy on my husband."

Overheard in Washington, D.C.:

"I know the first couple is from Arkansas, but I still can't believe their names are Hill and Billy."

A motorist driving down a dirt road noticed a boy up ahead who was running furiously with three dogs barking at his heels. He drove past them, pushed the car door open, and yelled, "Get in! Get in!"

"Gee, thanks mister," answered the boy, climbing in. "Most people won't offer a ride when they see I have three dogs."

Q. What are the three most difficult years for a redneck?

A. Second grade.

A highway patrol officer stopped a motorist on a stretch of road.

"Don't you know what a flashing light means, mister?" he asked.

"Yes, sir," replied the motorist.

"Well, then, why didn't you pull over immediately?"

"I would have, but last month my wife ran off with a policeman. I was afraid you were bringing her back."

Will bought a jigsaw puzzle and brought it home to work on. After two solid weeks he finally finished. Proudly, he told Johnny about his accomplishment.

"It took me just two weeks to finish it," he announced.

"Is that good?" asked Johnny.

"Sure is," replied Will. "Look—here on the box it says, 'two to four years.'"

A traffic cop approached Cyrus, who he had just pulled over for speeding.

"Do you have any ID?" he asked.

"About what?" replied Cyrus.

Q. Why did the redneck buy two CB radios?

A. So he could talk to himself.

Tully invited Preacher Perkins and Preacher Smith over to dinner one night. His wife prepared chicken, and the two guests ate one bird each. Following dinner, Tully took the two preachers around for a tour of his property. As they passed the henhouse, a rooster crowed as loud as could be.

"That rooster seems mighty proud of himself," said Preacher Perkins.

"Well, I guess he has a reason," said Tully. "After all, he has two children in the ministry."

Jittery Aunt Minnie rushed in to see Doctor Jones and gasped, "I just read a newspaper article that said sleeping outdoors will cure insomnia. Is that true?"

After giving it a moment's thought, the doctor replied, "Well, yes it is, but I think sleeping indoors will do it just as well."

A census taker approached the farmhouse and knocked on the door.

"Can you tell me how many people live here?" he asked Aunt Minnie when she answered the door.

"Well," she replied, "there's me and pa, Billy Joe, Bubba, Moose, Ellie May, Norma Jean, Thelma. . . "

"Hold on," said the census taker. "I don't need names, just numbers."

"We don't use numbers," said Aunt Minnie. "We ain't run out of names yet."

# YOU KNOW YOU'RE A REDNECK IF...

. . . your saddle costs more than your house.

. . . the furniture store in town only sells gun racks.

. . . your town's chief industry is whittling.

. . . the mall in your town is anchored by a blacksmith shop.

. . . at family gatherings the conversation usually turns to sump pumps.

. . . the rabbit ears on your TV come from a real rabbit.

. . . your town's department store mannequin is chewing tobacco.

A visitor walking down the road stopped by a farmer in the field.

"Excuse me," he said. "Do you happen to know what time it is?"

"Just a minute," replied the farmer. He walked over to a nearby cow, crouched down beside it, and gently lifted up the cow's udder.

"Ten to one," he said.

"That's incredible," exclaimed the man. "How can you tell time by feeling a cow's udder?"

"Come over here and I'll show you," said the farmer. "If you crouch down like this and lift the udder, you can just make out the church clock on the other side of the valley."

Bob was tickled pink to be sitting in his father-in-law's seat on the fifty-yard line for the Georgia-Auburn football game. He had arrived early to savor every moment, and now the stadium was filling up. A man sat down two seats away and unloaded his coat, cooler, hat, and bag on the seat next to him. Bob was impressed that the man had two precious seats, and was casually using one for storage. After a few minutes Bob leaned over and said, "It's pretty good that at these prices you can use a seat just to put your stuff on."

"It's my wife's seat," the man replied, "but she died."

"Oh, I'm terribly sorry to hear that," Bob lamented. "Couldn't you give the seat to one of your relatives?"

"Well, I tried," the man nodded. "But they're all at the funeral."

Bobby was at the train station in Alexandria, Louisiana saying good-bye to his father, the area's wealthiest planter. "Now Bobby, make sure you write to me and your mamma when you get down to Tulane."

Bobby nodded.

"And I want you to have enough money for school and your friends and all." With that, the planter pressed twenty thousand dollars into Bobby's hands and urged him onto the train.

Bobby had such a good time in New Orleans that he never did get around to enrolling. But with the partying and all, he quickly ran through the money, and was on the phone to his father.

"How is school going, son?" his father asked.

"Just fine, Daddy. I'm studying hard and I've joined a fraternity and made some nice friends. Tulane is amazing, Daddy. Why, they even have special study down here to teach dogs to read and write."

"Amazing! You mean like our coon hounds or Old Blue?"

"Exactly, Daddy. In fact, I was thinking that maybe we could put Old Blue in the program," suggested Bobby. "But it's expensive. Twenty thousand dollars."

"Well, it is a fact that he is the smartest dog I ever owned," said the planter. "Let's do it. I'll send him down on the train tomorrow and wire you the money."

When the dog arrived, Bobby left him in the back yard of the fraternity and proceeded to party his way through the money. Soon, he had exhausted the funds and had to call home again.

"How you and Old Blue doing, son?"

"Just fine, Daddy. I'm getting good grades and Old Blue is at the top of his class. Next week they are taking the top three dogs and teaching them how to talk. And, Daddy, Old Blue is one of them. But it'll cost another twenty thousand dollars."

"Hang the expense, son. Old Blue talking—why, just think of it. A check is on the way."

The predictable happened and Bobby was again broke. As he prepared to go home for Thanksgiving, he desperately tried to figure out how to explain the sixty thousand dollars. Then he got an idea.

That afternoon, when Bobby stepped off the train in Alexandria, his father was there to greet him.

"Where's Old Blue?" he asked.

Bobby shook his head. "I can't talk about it now, Daddy."

On the ride home, Bobby finally spoke again.

"So there we were on the train. Old Blue looked up from reading the *Wall Street Journal* and said how he was looking forward to having a long conversation with you after all these years. Then he said 'I want to ask your Daddy about those times when Emmie Sue, the waitress from town, would sneak in the back door at night and climb the stairs to his bedroom. I want to ask him what went on.'"

The planter's knuckles got white as he tightened his hands on the wheel. "Well, son, I hope you did the right thing."

"Yessir, I did. I shot that dog."

Tom and his wife were barreling down the back road when they heard a siren whine from a patrol car coming up behind them. Tom pulled over to the side of the road and presently

a stocky state trooper ambled up alongside the pickup. The trooper removed his sunglasses and peered in at the two.

"Moving along at a pretty good clip, weren't you? Don't you know the speed limit along here is forty-five. You must've been doing seventy."

Tom shook his head. "No, sir. I was going along at forty-five and then I speeded up for a moment to miss a cow that was crossing the road."

The trooper looked at Tom's wife who shook her head. "He was doing seventy-two, officer."

Tom whirled on his wife. "What do you mean by going on like that?" he snarled. "Why can't you ever support me when I say something?"

The trooper looked down at Tom. "You know, it's against the law to be driving without a seatbelt on, mister. And you don't have yours on."

"Oh, it was on when I was driving, officer," Tom protested. "I just loosened it now to get my wallet and driver's license out for you."

The trooper looked over at Tom's wife. "That right, ma'am?"

Again, Tom's wife shook her head. "He wasn't wearing his seatbelt when we were driving."

Tom turned to his wife and shouted, "Why'n the hell don't you ever back me up? Thirty-two years we've been married and you always contradict me."

The trooper was taken aback by Tom's shouting. "Your husband always yell at you like that, ma'am?" he asked.

She shook her head and sweetly replied, "Just when he's been drinking."

Billy and his pregnant wife, Ellen, were farmers in Alabama and lived miles and miles from the nearest town. One evening, while he and his wife were finishing up in the barn, the labor pains began. Collapsing on a bale of hay, Ellen cried out, "I can't move, Billy. Call the doctor in town. The baby's coming!"

Billy raced to the house and dialed the doctor, who said he'd be there in twenty minutes. He told Billy to keep his wife warm and not try to move her. Billy rushed back to the barn and, minutes later, the doctor arrived. Directing Billy to hold a light over the prostrate woman, the doctor swiftly performed his ministrations.

"Hold the light a little closer now, Billy," the doctor ordered. "There! I'd like to congratulate you. You're the father of a beautiful baby boy!"

"Oh, thank you so much, Doctor," Billy gasped emotionally.

"Wait a minute, hold the light a little closer again," instructed the doctor. "Well, well! Look here. Now you're the father of two brand new baby boys." The doctor proudly held up the latest arrival.

"Well, golly, Doctor," said Billy, backing away to a corner of the barn.

"Hey, Billy, bring the light a little closer. Make that three boys!" the doctor said triumphantly, as he pulled another little head through.

"Doc, I'm overwhelmed," Billy murmured and began to turn the light out.

*"You're right. That certainly does look like Elvis on the next cloud, doesn't it?"*

"Not so fast, Billy. Bring the lamp back over," the doctor motioning to Billy.

"Excuse me, Doctor," Billy demurred, staying where he was. "But don't you think it might be the light that keeps attracting them?"

Aunt Sue and Uncle Jem were at a country bar enjoying a drink. Uncle Jem was munching on some pretzels, but Aunt Sue didn't touch a single one. Thinking this a bit unusual, the bartender asked her if she'd like one.

"Sure," she answered. "I'm just waiting for him to finish using the teeth."

Q. Why does it take a redneck five days to wash his basement windows?

A. He needs four-and-a-half days to dig the holes for the ladder.

An Arkansas farmer walked into the barber shop and was quickly seated. "I need a nice haircut, Lem," the farmer said as he sat down. "I'm making my first trip to Washington."

"Really!" said the barber. "Are you driving up there."

"Nope, we're flying out of Memphis. On Northwest."

"Northwest is the lousiest!" exclaimed the barber. "Why, you'll be crammed in, three to a row. They never leave on time. Terrible food. They're the pits."

"So, where you staying in Washington?" asked Lem as he snipped away.

"We're staying at the Sheraton," the farmer replied.

"Oh, the worst!" Lem commented. "Tiny rooms, no amenities. Haughty attitude at the desk. Long waits for the elevators. Big mistake," he said punctuating the air with his scissors.

"What are you going to do in D.C.?" Lem continued.

"Well, we're looking forward to touring the White House and maybe meeting the President."

"Hah, do you know what you're getting into!?" the barber shouted. "A three hour wait outside. Then once you're in there are slow lines from one public room to another. And forget about even seeing the President." With that he gave a final snip with the scissors and whipped off the sheet.

Bob hurriedly paid and left. Two months later he was back in the barber shop.

"So how was your trip? Wasn't Northwest really Northworst?"

"Not at all," said the farmer. "They couldn't have been nicer. They even upgraded us to first class. And we had a great meal."

"Well, I'm sure the hotel was just as bad as I said. Right?"

"No, the same thing happened there. They upgraded us to a huge suite with a private elevator. And there was even a bottle of champagne waiting for us in the room."

"Hmmm. I'll bet the White House tour was terrible though."

"No, it was wonderful. We had a private tour and then we happened to meet the President who was passing through."

The barber was impressed. "Really? Did he say anything to you?"

"Yes, he said, 'Where'd you get that lousy haircut?'"

To be frank, I find these people anything but deep. I was in Birmingham, Alabama, working a small comedy club called 'I Don't Get It'.

*Dennis Miller*

Harley worked at the saw mill next to Luke, a fellow worker who was a born-again Christian. Practically the only thing Luke talked about was leading the good life, so that when his Judgment Day arrived he'd be ready. Luke was constantly lecturing Harley and reminding him that he could not live forever. "Harley, you know you should settle down and raise a good family and start attending church regularly, don't you?" Harley just nodded, since he had heard all this before.

"Why, Harley, don't you hear that 'tick, tick, tick'?" asked Luke, pointing to the big clock at the end of the mill. "Don't you know what day every tick brings us closer and closer to?"

Harley looked up, "Yeh, pay day."

A blind redneck and his Seeing Eye dog walked into a store. He grabbed the dog by the tail, picked him up over his head, and started swinging him around in a circle. The puzzled clerk looked at him and asked, "Can I get you anything?"

"No thanks," replied the man. "I'm just looking around."

Frank was an ex-major leaguer, but he had worked in the mines in West Virginia for the past thirty years. Now in his 70s, he was in poor health and down on his luck, and needed an operation. He asked around and was finally directed to the most respected and expensive specialist in town.

"Doctor, I've been told that I need this expensive operation," Frank explained.

"I'm afraid it'll cost you twenty thousand dollars. In advance," replied the doctor.

"What! But, Doctor, c'mon, times are tough, I don't make the big bucks that I did when I was playing ball!"

"I'll tell you what I'll do," the doctor responded. "I used to be a big fan of yours. I'll call it a thousand and you send me one of your old uniforms."

"That's still too steep," protested Frank.

They haggled back and forth, and finally settled on fifty dollars and the baseball cap the old timer wore in the World Series.

"At that price, I might as well do it for free!" said the doctor, shaking his head. "Tell me, if you knew I was the most expensive doctor in town, and you knew you couldn't afford it, why did you come here?"

"Hey, Doctor," replied Frank, "where my health is concerned, money is no object."

Q. What's the difference between a redneck grandmother and an elephant?

A. About seven pounds.

There were probably just as many church-going people in town that attended the First Baptist Church as avoided it, and the reason was one in the same—Minister Jackson. Minister Jackson was known for his long sermons that sometimes went on for several hours extolling the virtues of following the ten commandments and dwelling at great length on the fires of damnation. This was one of the those Sunday mornings and the minister was rolling on non-stop for forty-five minutes with no sign of coming to a conclusion. Finally, he paused to catch his breath. He mopped his brow and rolled his eyes heavenward. "And what shall I say next?" he intoned.

A voice yelled out from the back of the church, "How about an 'amen'?"

"Hey, Sam," the farmer yelled out to his hired hand, "Did you take the new horse out and shod him like I asked?"

"Did you say 'shod'?"

"Yeah, what did you think I said?"

"I thought you said 'shot'. I just finished burying him!"

"Hey, Billy, did you make any money with your tobacco crop last season?"

"Are you kidding! I didn't even make enough to keep me in cigarettes."

Q. What did the redneck do when he found out he was being promoted from second grade to third grade?

A. He got so excited, he cut himself shaving.

Billy Bob stopped at the Do Drop Inn, a small low-rent hotel on the outskirts of town. Hauling his suitcase up the stairs, he opened his door, pulled the light chain, and started to unpack. Then he noticed that there was a steady and annoying 'drip drip drip' coming from the bottom of the sink in the corner. Billy Bob picked up the phone and called down to the front desk. When the desk clerk answered, Billy Bob said, "This is room 319. What about a leak in my sink?"

The clerk barely hesitated before replying, "Oh, go right ahead."

Q. What did the redneck mother say when her daughter told her she was pregnant?

A. "Are you sure it's yours?"

Reverend Billy, founder and pastor of his own church, was studying the Bible in his house when suddenly the Lord appeared. The shining vision spoke to Reverend Billy and said "Because you have done such a good job with your church here in Georgia, I am here to grant you three wishes."

Billy was astonished. "Lord, I'm almost speechless, but let me think."

The Lord thundered, "What is your first wish?"

"I'd like you to eliminate all the pain and suffering in the world."

"Done," said the Heavenly voice. "Your second wish?"

Billy thought for a few seconds. "Well, we have all these big-city tourists coming through here calling us dumb, ignorant, redneck white trash and I'd like to shut them up once and for all. Can you build me a magnificent cathedral here in Cowslip?"

The Lord waved His hand. "There you are, Reverend Billy, more magnificent than St. Paul's Cathedral. Now what is your last wish?"

"Well, I'd like you to get rid of those M&M's, if you don't mind."

The Lord was silent for a heavenly second and then said, "That is a strange request, Reverend Billy, so let me make sure I have this straight. You mean those little chocolate candies with the thin, crisp candy shell?"

Billy nodded vigorously. "That's right, my Lord. M&M's."

"I can do it certainly, but why?"

"Because they're so hard to peel."

Q. What do you call two 500 pound women sitting at a bar?

A. A half-ton pick up.

A truck driver was delivering bread to a diner on the outskirts of Valdosta. When he walked in, the place was almost entirely filled with members of a motorcycle gang. All he saw were chains, black leather, tattoos, and big, rugged-looking guys. With his arms full of bread trays, the driver failed to see the outstretched leg of one of the cyclists, and he stumbled and almost dropped his stack of loaves. Muttering to himself, he quickly delivered his bread and got the receipt. As he turned to leave, he stopped and yelled, "You motorcycle guys are a bunch a lily-livered jerks and a bunch of wusses!" He then bolted out the door, ran to his truck, and tore off down the road.

The cycle gang just sneered at the running figure and they all went back to their lunches. When they were through and at the cash register, one of them said to the waitress, "That pathetic jerk who ran out of here wasn't much of a man, was he?"

The waitress handed his change back and replied, "No, he wasn't. And he wasn't much of a driver, either. I saw him run over twenty Harleys on his way out of the parking lot."

"Say, Sally," asked her neighbor Joleen, "Why do they only have sex education classes two days a week down at the school?"

"Because the other three days they use the mule for driver's ed."


A salesman, who was driving past a farm while out on a call, was amazed to see a farmer lifting a large pig to the branch of an apple tree. Pulling over, he watched the pig bite an apple off the branch. The farmer put the pig down on the ground, where the animal continued eating his prize. The farmer repeated with another pig, then a third and a fourth. Finally, unable to contain himself any longer, the salesman went up to the farmer.

"Excuse me," he said, "but wouldn't it be a lot easier if *you* climbed up and picked the apples, then gave them to the pigs?"

"I don't know," replied the farmer, reaching for another porker. "What would be the big advantage to doin' that?"

"Well," answered the salesman, "for one thing, it would save a lot of time."

"Could be," said the farmer. "But then again, what's time to a pig?"


In Alabama, they think high cholesterol is some sort of religious holiday.

*"Sit still, Melanie, you're throwing me off balance."*

Q. Who has the right of way when four cars come up to a four way stop at the same time?

A. The pickup truck with the gun rack and the bumper sticker that reads "Guns don't kill people. I do."

A visitor to Alabama was out hunting ducks without having much success. Finally, after eight long hours, he managed to shoot one. As luck would have it, the duck fell to earth just on the other side of a fence, on the property of a nearby farmer. As the hunter scaled the fence to get his prize, the farmer appeared.

"What do you think you're doing?" asked the farmer.

"I'm just getting my duck," replied the hunter. "When I shot it, it fell inside your fence."

"Sorry," said the farmer. "You can't have it. If it fell on my property, it belongs to me."

"But you don't understand," said the hunter. "I've been out here eight hours without any luck. This is the only duck I shot. I've got to have it."

"Sorry," repeated the farmer, "but that's the law."

"That's crazy," said the hunter. "Isn't there some way we can work it out so I can keep the duck?"

"Well," replied the farmer, "if it means so much to you, I suppose we could settle this problem the way men do here in Alabama."

"How's that?" asked the hunter.

"Well, we stand facing each other, then take turns kicking each other in the groin. The last one to remain standing is the winner. If you'd like, we can do that to decide who gets the duck."

The hunter was flabbergasted, but after mulling over the hours he had wasted without anything to show for it, he finally agreed to the contest, determined to come away with his prize.

"Fine," said the farmer. "Now, since it's my property, I get to go first."

Without giving the hunter a chance to reply, the farmer pulled his leg back and delivered a tremendous kick to the hunter's groin. The hunter flew into the air with an agonizing scream, then came down to earth, where he proceeded to roll around on the ground with tears of pain pouring from his eyes. After several minutes of unbelievable agony, he somehow managed to get one knee under him, then another. Still moaning in pain, he slowly got up on one leg, then with a final Herculean burst of effort, pulled himself up on both legs.

Gazing at the farmer through teary eyes, with both legs wobbling underneath him, the hunter said, "Well, I did it. Now it's my turn."

"Naw," said the farmer, walking away with a shrug. "You can keep the duck."

Two country bumpkins had just pulled off a daring bank robbery, and were speeding away from the bank. Pauly, the driver, yelled to Ken, his accomplice, to watch and see if the cops were following them.

"How will I know if it's the cops?" asked Ken.

"Easy," replied Pauly. "They'll have their flashers on."

Ken turned around to look out the window. Gazing down the road, he said, "Yes, no, yes, no, yes, no..."

I don't like dating rednecks because you can't do anything cultural with them. Take them to an art gallery and they'll say, "This is crap."

"That's a Picasso," I reply.

"What about this bunch of damn squiggles?"

"That's a Kandinsky."

"All right, well, like in this one the guy's got a pencil neck, his nose is upside down, and his eyes are on the same side of his head."

"That's a mirror."

*Pam Stone*

A salesman, driving to his next appointment, happened to look out the window of his car and was amazed to see a three-legged chicken running along next to him. Although the car was traveling at forty miles per hour, the chicken was keeping up with it. The salesman accelerated to fifty, but the chicken also sped up to keep pace with him.

The incredulous salesman gunned his car till he was going sixty miles per hour. Looking out the window, he saw the chicken still beside him. All of a sudden, the chicken shot ahead, leaving the car in a cloud of dust. The salesman, clearly shaken, pulled over to the side of the road. Trying to understand what he had seen, he noticed a farmer nearby. Still dazed, he explained to the farmer what had occurred.

"Oh, yeah," the farmer said. "That's one of my chickens. You see, my wife and I have one son, and each of us likes a drumstick when we have chicken for dinner. So, the only solution I could think of was to breed three-legged chickens."

"That's unbelievable," said the salesman. "How do they taste?"

"Don't know," replied the farmer. "Never been able to catch one."

Frank and Billy Bob were out hiking in the woods when Frank got bit on the rear by a rattlesnake.

"Wait here," yelled Billy Bob. "I'll go get a doctor and find out what to do."

Billy Bob ran ten miles to the nearest town and rushed into a doctor's office.

"Doc, you've gotta come quick," he said breathlessly. "My best friend's been bitten by a rattlesnake."

"I'm sorry," replied the doctor, "but I'm very busy right now and can't come with you. But I'll tell you what to do. Take a small knife and cut an X in each one of the puncture marks. Then suck out the poison and spit it out until it's all gone from the wound. Your friend should be okay after that."

Billy Bob ran back the ten miles to Frank, and found him laying on the ground, writhing in pain.

"Well," groaned Frank, "what did the doctor say?"

"He said you're gonna die," replied Billy Bob.

Q. Why does it take seven people to give a redneck a shower?

A. Three to hold him down, and four to spit on him.

Beau and his girlfriend were out for a stroll in the fields when they came across a cow and a calf rubbing noses.

"Boy," said Beau, "that sight sure makes me want to do the same."

"Well, go ahead," said his girlfriend. "It's your cow."

Herb went to visit his cousin Lester in the country. As he pulled up to Lester's farm, he was amazed to see a pig with a wooden leg running around the property. Seeing his cousin, Herb asked, "Does that pig really have a wooden leg?"

"Sure does," answered Lester. "Let me explain. That's George, who's probably the smartest pig in the entire county. Two years ago, George had a book of poetry published by a major publishing house. Ever since then, he's been writing a financial column for the local newspaper."

"That's kind of hard to believe," exclaimed his cousin.

"Well, there's more," continued Lester. "Two weeks ago, the house caught on fire, and George dialed 911, then ran inside and rescued Mom and baby Jessica."

"That's unbelievable," his cousin marveled. "But I still don't understand why George has a wooden leg."

"With a pig like that," explained Lester, "you don't eat him all at once."

For years, Rufus had been dealing with the same bank in town and, being illiterate, had always signed his checks with an X. One day, the bank teller noticed two X's instead of one. Asked the reason for the change, Rufus replied, "Well, I decided to start using my middle name."

Johnny and Sammy were working in the fields one day when they noticed a funeral procession passing by.

"I wonder who died," said Johnny.

"I'm not sure," replied Sammy, "but I think it's the fella in the first car."

A farmer with twenty lazy hired workers on his farm tried to come up with a plan to cure them of their bad work habits.

"Men," he announced one morning, "I have a nice easy job for the laziest one of you. Will the laziest man step forward."

Nineteen of the twenty men promptly stepped forward.

The farmer approached the one remaining man.

"Why didn't you step forward with the rest, Bob?" he asked.

"Too much trouble," was the reply.

Q. What's the most popular redneck pick-up line?

A. Nice tooth.

*"When you said, 'Let's go for a ride on my hog,'
I thought you had a motorcycle."*

"What's that piece of string around your finger for?" asked
Zeb.

"My wife put it there to remind me to mail a letter," answered Buford.

"Well, did you mail it?"

"No. She forgot to give it to me."

Bill was visiting the big city for the first time, and staying at a large hotel. Before going to bed for the night, he asked the clerk what time meals were served.

"Breakfast is served from seven to eleven," the clerk replied. "Lunch from twelve to three and supper from four to eight."

"Gosh," replied Bill, "don't leave much time for sightseein', do it?"

"Man," said Fred stretching out his hands, "did I catch a fish the other day! It was enormous. It was t-h-i-s long. Why, I never saw such a fish!"

"That I believe," replied Al.

As Sally walked to her new job, late again, her boss approached her.

"You're late again," she said. "Don't you know what time we start work around here?"

"Nope," replied Sally. "They're already working whenever I get here."

Q. What happens when you play country music backwards?

A. You get your job back, your wife back, your truck back, and your dog back.

A slick salesman was passing through a small Mississippi town selling an elixir he said would make men live to ripe old ages. A small crowd had gathered in the town square to hear his talk.

"Look at me," he said. "I take this tonic every day and I'm healthy as can be at over three hundred years of age."

A woman in the gathering turned to the salesman's young assistant.

"Is he really as old as he said?" she asked.

"I can't really say," was the reply. "I've only known him for a hundred years."

Q. Why did the redneck highway construction worker lose his job?

A. Someone invented a shovel that stands up on its own.

Porter and his wife, Betty Sue, were a pair of laid-back farmers. One day they were sitting on their porch when a funeral procession passed by. Porter, who was whittling on a piece of wood, observed, "I reckon old man Taylor's having just about the biggest funeral ever seen in these here parts."

"A pretty good-sized one, is it?" asked Betty Sue, who was rocking and knitting.

"Sure is," replied Porter.

"I sure would like to see it," continued Betty Sue. "It's a shame I ain't facing that way."

"Oh, what a funny looking cow," said the sweet young thing from Atlanta, visiting a farm for the first time. "Why doesn't it have any horns?"

"Well, there are many reasons why a cow doesn't have horns," answered the farmer. "Some are born without horns and don't get any until they're much older. Others are dehorned when they're young. Still other breeds just don't have any at all."

The farmer paused for a moment. "But the chief reason this cow doesn't have any horns is because it's a horse."

Q. Why does a redneck go to a family funeral?

A. To meet women.

Dickie was in agony laying in a hospital bed after falling off his tractor.

"Ask him what his name is so we can notify his family," the doctor instucted the nurse.

"He said not to bother," replied the nurse. "His family knows his name."

The day a redneck will clean his house is when Sears comes out with a riding vacuum cleaner.

A vacationing family was enjoying itself swimming in the lake after a holiday meal when all of a sudden the husband saw someone struggling in the water. Catching a glimpse of the woman's face, he called out to young Johnny, who happened to be nearby, "My wife is drowning! I'll give you a hundred dollars if you can save her!"

In a flash, Johnny swam out to the woman, grabbed her around the waist and pulled her back to shore. Approaching the husband, he said, "Well, how about that hundred dollars?"

The man's face turned red with embarrassment as he looked at the recovering woman.

"Oh," he gasped, "when I made the offer, I thought it was my wife who was drowning. But now, I see, it was actually my mother-in-law."

"Just my luck," muttered Johnny, reaching his hand into his pocket. "How much do I owe you?"


The school teacher told young Ernest a riddle.

"If there were three crows sitting on a fence," she said, "and I shot one, how many would be left?"

"Two left," replied Ernest.

"I'm afraid you don't get the point," said the teacher. "Let me repeat the riddle. There were three crows sitting on a fence. Then I shot one. How many would be left?"

"Two left," repeated Ernest.

"No," corrected the teacher. "None would be left, because if I shot one, the other two would fly away."

"That's what I've been saying," Ernest protested. "Two left."

I was just in Branson, Missouri. That place is Las Vegas for people without teeth. I felt like Mark Fuhrman at the Apollo Theater.

*Dennis Miller*

Ellie May went to the dentist to have her tooth extracted.

"How much do you charge to pull a tooth?" she asked.

"Fifty dollars," replied the dentist.

"Gee, that's a lot of money for only a few seconds work," complained Ellie May.

"Well," suggested the dentist, "I could do it v-e-r-y s-l-o-w-l-y."

Lovestruck Hank told his girl that if she didn't marry him, he'd get a rope and hang himself right in front of her home.

"Oh, please don't do that," she pleaded. "You know my pa doesn't want you hanging around here."

"Doctor," said Jake, "I got a pain here in my right leg."

"There's nothing I can do for you," explained the doctor. "It's due to old age."

"That's ridiculous," answered Jake. "My left leg is just as old as my right one and it don't hurt me at all."

Hal went to see his family doctor. "I'm so unhappy, Doc. I can't find a woman to make my life complete."

"I've got a suggestion," said the doctor. "Why don't you advertise in one of those singles columns in the Atlanta paper. Look for a woman who likes to do the same things you like to do."

"That don't make no sense," scoffed Hal. "What am I gonna do with a woman who likes to whistle at girls?"

Dwight stopped at a bar on his way home. After he got a beer, he wandered around and noticed a large fish tank near the jukebox. The sign posted near it read DANGEROUS PIRANHA. DO NOT TOUCH! Not believing the sign, Dwight stuck his hand in and wiggled his finger.

"Hey," yelled the bartender. "Can't you read? Yesterday one of those fish bit my finger off."

"Which one?" asked Dwight.

"How should I know? All those fish look the same to me."

Ray and Charlie were hiking in the forest when they came upon a giant grizzly bear. As the seven-foot-tall bear started growling at them, Ray took off his shoes and started putting on his sneakers.

"What are you doing?" asked Charlie. "Why are you putting your sneakers on? You'll never outrun a bear!"

"Don't have to," replied Ray. "Just have to outrun you."

Woody and George were driving their truck over the back roads of the south when they came to an overpass with a sign on it that read CLEARANCE 11' 3". They got out and measured their rig and found that it was 12' 5" tall.

"What do you think?" asked Woody.

"Not a cop in sight," said George. "Let's take a chance."

There are two kinds of guys in the South—good ole boys and rednecks. The difference is good ole boys may raise livestock, rednecks get emotionally involved.

*Blake Clark*

Q. What's the difference between a redneck and a cat?

A. One lies on the couch losing his hair, and the other is your house pet.

A redneck cleaning out his barn fell through the floor into the manure storeroom.

"Fire!" he yelled.

When his son came and pulled him out, he asked, "Why did you yell 'fire'?"

The farmer replied, "Would you have come if I'da yelled 'Manure'?"

Donny: "Does your dog have a good pedigree?"

Vann: "I'll say. It's so good, if he could talk, he wouldn't speak to either one of us."

A kindly old farmer found young Tyson sitting on the side of the road, looking as sad as could be. Next to him was a load of hay which had overturned in the road.

"Come back to the house with me," said the farmer. "If you have a bite of dinner with me and my family, things won't seem so bad."

"Oh, no," said Tyson. "I don't think my pa would like that."

"Nonsense," said the farmer. "By the way, where is your father?"

"Under the hay," answered Tyson.

The teacher asked her class to write a composition telling what they would do if they had five million dollars. Every student except Fannie started writing immediately. After ten minutes, the teacher collected the papers, only to find Fannie had handed in a blank sheet.

"What's this?" asked the teacher. "Everyone else has written at least two pages, but you've done nothing."

"Well," replied Fannie, "that's what I would do if I had five million dollars."

Jesse took his wife to the local airfield for their first airplane ride. When he asked about the rates for a short trip, he was informed a ten-minute ride over the countryside would cost one hundred dollars.

Jesse was appalled.

"That's ten dollars a minute," he complained. "Don't you have anything cheaper?"

"Tell you what I'll do," replied the pilot. "Since you want to go up so badly, I'll take the two of you up for nothing if you'll agree not to say a single word the entire time we're up in the air. If you say anything at all, it'll cost you the full price."

Jesse talked it over with his wife, and they agreed to the terms.

With the couple tucked into the plane, the pilot took off over the countryside. When the plane reached an altitude of 3,000 feet, he proceeded to try to make the couple break their silence. He performed a tail spin, two loop-the-loops, and three barrel rolls, but all to no avail. Not a single word was spoken.

Upon landing, the pilot reached out to shake Jesse's hand.

"Well," he said, "you won fair and square. The ride's yours free of charge. Not too many people going up for the first time could have gone through what you did without crying out."

"I guess so," said Jesse proudly, "but to tell you the truth, you almost got me there once, when my old lady fell out."

The farmer whose pig was killed by the speeding motorist was raving mad.

"Don't worry," said the driver, "I'll replace your pig."

"You can't," growled the farmer, "you ain't fat enough."

Jake, one half of the most inept counterfeiting team around, got out of the Georgia state prison and was met by his brother, Willie, who was released six months earlier.

"Jake, we are back in business. I've got some great plates made and all we have to do is get these bills printed up and we are rich men!"

Jake beamed. "Let's go, Willie. I know where there is some paper stored."

Three days later, the brothers had a newly minted stack of bills several feet high. Surveying their potential fortune, Jake examined one if the bills closely. "Willie, you idiot! These bills don't have '$20' on them. They say '$18.' What are we supposed to do with a stack of '$18' bills?"

Willie thought for a moment and then brightened, "Let's take 'em to South Georgia. They won't know the difference down there."

The two brothers drove south and three hours later pulled into a gas station to fill up. When they were through, Willie handed the attendant two eighteen dollar bills. "Say, pardner, can I get change for that second bill?"

"No problem, sir," the attendant replied. "Do you want two nine dollar bills or three sixes?"

Q. What did the absent-minded redneck say when he found a rope?

A. Well, I've either found a rope or lost a horse.


Edie: "Where do ears of corn come from, Mama?"

Mama: "Why honey, the stalk brings them."


Parker didn't have much success fishing, so on the way home he stopped by the fish market.

"Say, Sam," he said, "stand over by the stand and throw me a couple of your biggest trout."

"Throw 'em?" asked Sam. "Why don't you just take 'em yourself?"

"Well," replied Parker, "when I get home the wife's gonna ask me how many fish I caught today. I may not be such a good fisherman, but I sure ain't no liar."


Patsy was back home for the holidays, the first in her family ever to make it to college. One day she said to her mother, "Momma, can I tell you a narrative?"

"What's a narrative?" she asked.

"A narrative is a tale," replied Patsy.

That night, before going to bed, Patsy said, "Can I extinguish the light, Momma?"

"What does extinguish mean?" she asked.

"Extinguish means put out," answered her daughter.

A couple days later, Patsy's momma was having some neighbors over for tea when the dog walked into the house.

"Patsy," she cried, "take that dog by the narrative and extinguish him."

Q. What did the redneck father do when Bubba said he wanted to marry his daughter?

A. He was so surprised, the gun fell right out of his hands.

After delivering a powerful sermon on the new morality, Reverend Tompkins asked all the virgins in the church to please stand up. Although there was a lot of stirring about, no one stood up. After about thirty seconds or so, a young woman with a baby in her arms got to her feet in the back of the church.

"I'm afraid you misunderstood," said the reverend. "I asked that only virgins stand up."

"Well," replied the woman, "you don't expect a three-month old baby to stand up by herself, do you?"

"Young Trent, who used to work for you, wants me to give him a job," said farmer Jones. "Is he steady?"

"If he was any steadier," replied farmer Hayes, "he'd be motionless."

The new town doctor, right out of medical school, was seeing one of his first patients.

"Before you came to see me, who was treating you for your problem?" he asked.

"Just old man Boyle down at the corner drugstore," replied Hattie.

Unable to hide his disdain for a lay person giving out medical advice, the doctor blurted out, "And just what kind of stupid advice did that incompetent old fool give you?"

"He told me to come and see you," answered Hattie.

A slightly inebriated redneck was searching diligently along the edge of the curb. A policeman approached him.

"What are you looking for?" asked the cop.

"I just lost fifty cents," replied Hollis.

"Where did you lose it?"

"About a half block down the street."

"Well, then, why in the world are you looking for it here?" asked the officer.

"Oh, the light's much better over here," answered Hollis.

A salesman at the general store was trying to persuade the farmer to buy a tractor.

"I'd rather spend my money on a cow," said the farmer.

"But think how silly you'd look riding around on a cow," replied the salesman.

"Not half as silly as I'd look trying to milk a tractor," responded the farmer.

The teacher was trying to explain the idea of antonyms to the class.

"Now, children, what is the opposite of sorrow?"

"Joy," answered Tommy.

"And what is the opposite of pleasure?"

"Pain," answered Rosalie.

"And what is the opposite of woe?"

"Giddyap," answered Billy Bob.

"Name five things that contain milk," asked the teacher.

"Butter, cheese, ice cream . . . and two cows," replied Fannie Mae.

The high-pressure vacuum cleaner salesman was forcing a home demonstration on Betty Sue. He took a large paper bag out of his case and proceeded to spill its contents all over the rug—coffee grounds, rocks, lint, and all kinds of dirt.

"Ma'am, I'll eat every bit of this stuff that this vacuum doesn't pick up," the salesman announced proudly.

Betty Sue got up to leave the room.

"Where are you going?" asked the salesman.

"To get a knife and fork," she replied. "We don't have electricity."

Jeff kept asking the pretty young manicurist at the barber shop for a date, but she repeatedly turned him down.

"But why won't you go out with me?" he finally asked.

"Because I'm engaged," replied the girl.

"What difference does that make?" said Jeff. "Ask your boyfriend."

"Why don't you ask him yourself?" she said. "He's shaving you."

Shopper: "How much are these tomatoes?"

Susie: "Ninety cents a pound."

Shopper: "Did you raise them yourself?"

Susie: "Sure did. Just yesterday they were eighty cents a pound."

"Did you hear about Tammy? She had triplets and two weeks later she had twins."

"That's impossible! How did it happen?"

"One of the triplets got lost."

Q. What does a redneck call a cow with no legs?

A. Ground beef.

# YOU KNOW YOU'RE A REDNECK IF...

. . . you put out a campfire by peeing on it.

. . . you use coupons to pay for your anniversary dinner.

. . . you'll walk a mile for a Camel, but won't walk twenty feet to take the trash out.

. . . you think rock music is made by hitting a boulder with a stick.

. . . you consider shooting yourself in the head to stop your headache.

. . . your kid was conceived at a rodeo.

. . . your child's first word was "Howdy."

. . . your belt buckle weighs more than your kid.

. . . even your dog eats chili for breakfast.

. . . the snowman in your yard is picking its teeth.

A priest with both arms in casts ran into Jimmy and Kathy, who were in town for some Saturday shopping. Jimmy inquired about the man's accident.

"Fell in the bathtub," explained the priest to the two, who both nodded and went on their way.

They had walked on for a bit before Jimmy finally spoke up, "Say, Kathy, what is a bathtub anyhow?"

"How would I know?" replied Kathy. "I'm not Catholic."

Wilson and David were out hunting and managed to bag a deer. They started to drag it by its tail back to their pickup truck more than a mile away. Unfortunately, the antlers kept catching in the weeds, making the going very difficult. After a couple of hours, they managed to drag the animal within a couple of hundred yards of the truck, where they met Billie Joe.

"Hey," said Billie Joe, "it's a lot easier if you drag the deer by the horns."

Wilson and David took his advice. A while later, Wilson turned to David.

"Billie Joe was right," he said. "It sure is a lot easier dragging this deer by its horns than by its tail."

"Yeah," replied David, "but have you noticed how far away from the truck we're getting?"

Q. What has eighty legs and three teeth?

A. The front row of a Billy Ray Cyrus concert.

Some of our alumni have thought we should recruit wider. We had been working Houston and East Texas hard. But I told them, 'Okay, we'll go out of state a little more.' So we started working West Texas.

*Bill Yeoman, University of Houston football coach*

Young Cal came home from Sunday school and his mother asked him what he learned.

"We learned about a great farmer named Solomon."

"I didn't know Solomon was a farmer," said his mother.

"Neither did I," replied Cal, "but teacher said he had three hundred and seventy cucumber vines."

A mule kicked a redneck's mother-in-law to death, and a huge crowd gathered for the woman's funeral.

"That old lady must really have been popular," remarked a passer-by.

"Heck no," replied Pickett. "She was the orneriest old lady in the county. All these people just want to buy the mule that was strong enough to outkick her!"

I love those slow-talking Southern girls. I was out with a Southern girl last night, took her so long to tell me she wasn't that kind of girl, she was.

*Woody Woodbury*

The obstetrician came into the waiting room to see Cross, who was waiting for his wife.

"Congratulations," he said. "Your wife is going to have twins."

Cross's face turned bright red as he jumped to his feet and started to leave the office.

"What's wrong?" the doctor inquired.

"Just wait until I get hold of that other guy," he raged.


Ditsy Baummortal went duck shooting with old Uncle George Terwilliger. A flock of ducks flew overhead and Uncle George took a potshot at them and one fell down on the beach. Dead. Ditsy walked over and looked at it.

"Hey, Uncle George," he said. "That was a waste of ammunition to shoot that duck. The fall alone would have killed it."

*"Senator" Ed Ford*


"How did Bubba lose the fingers on his right hand?" asked Ben.

"He put them in a horse's mouth to see how many teeth the horse had," answered Willie.

"And then what happened?"

"The horse closed his mouth to see how many fingers Bubba had."

*"Shhhh. Bunny on the lawn."*

Q. How many country singers does it take to screw in a light bulb?

A. Two. One to screw in the bulb and one to sing about how much he misses the old one.

Mickey and Larry got themselves all set for a fine day of hunting. They gathered their dogs, together with their ammunition and guns, and stayed out for eight hours, without a bit of luck. Leaving the woods at dusk, they looked around at all the other hunters carrying their prizes—ducks, geese, quail, and deer.

"Gee," said Mickey, "everyone else sure did okay hunting. What do you think we did wrong?"

"I don't know," answered Larry. "Maybe we didn't throw the dogs high enough."

Beauregard and Bubba were out fishing one day, and everything was going their way. The weather was beautiful and the fish were biting as fast they could get their hooks into the water. After filling up their boat with fish, they decided to head for shore.

"Wait," said Bubba. "Let's mark this spot so we'll know where to come next time."

"No problem," assured Beauregard. He dove over the side, and painted a big black X on the bottom of the boat.

They headed back to shore, and began carrying their catch to their car. Just then, Bubba stopped dead in his tracks.

"What's the matter?" asked Beauregard.

"I just realized," said Bubba, "what if we don't get the same boat next time?"

Randy's old grandma was sitting on her porch, rocking away in her rocker. All of a sudden, a fairy godmother appeared in a beautiful gown and told her she could have any three wishes she wants.

Randy's grandmother thought for a while. "I guess I'd like to be really, really rich."

The fairy godmother waved her wand, and grandma's rocking chair turned into solid gold.

"And I guess I wouldn't mind being young and beautiful."

Another wave, and she was changed into a gorgeous young girl.

"You still have one more wish," said the fairy godmother. Just then, a mangy old cat walked across the porch in front of them.

"Can you change him into a handsome young prince?" asked grandma.

A third wave, and the most gorgeous young man she'd ever seen appeared in front of her.

With a smile, the young Adonis walked across the porch and smiled at her. "Now, aren't you sorry you had me fixed?"

Q. Why don't redneck factory workers get coffee breaks?

A. It takes too long to re-train them.

"Why have you chosen this career for yourself?" the well-dressed woman asked Russell.

"Well, ma'am," he replied, "I always dreamed of making a million dollars in farming, just like my paw."

"Oh, your father made a million dollars in farming?" asked the woman.

"Nope," answered Russell. "But he always dreamed of it."

An old farmer named Bob walked into a bar, sat down, and put his legless dog on the stool next to him. The bartender poured a beer for Bob, and then, to make conversation, asked the dog's name.

"He don't have no name," replied Bob.

The bartender, not sure if he heard him right, asked again, "Come on, Bob, what's his name?"

"I told you. He don't have no name."

"I don't believe you," said the bartender. "Every dog has a name."

"Not this one," drawled Bob. "What good is a name? Can't come when I call him."

I pull into this town called Weedpatch. I check into the Weedpatch Hotel, and they give me a *Key* magazine with all the events going on in town. I open it up—there's a picture of me checking into the Weedpatch Hotel.

*Monica Piper*

# DID YOU HEAR ABOUT...

The redneck who left his estate in trust for his wife? She can't touch it until she's thirteen.

The redneck who had body odor on one side only? He didn't know where to buy Left Guard.

The two redneck hunters? They were driving in their pickup when they came to a sign that said BEAR LEFT. So they went home.

The redneck farmer who broke up with his girlfriend, the daughter of a tractor salesman? She got a John Deere letter.

The redneck who urinated in a wheat field and was immediately arrested by a state trooper? He was charged with "Going against the grain."

The town in North Carolina that is so small, they're still excited about the wheel.

Henry heard about a vacation cruise that only cost one hundred dollars. After he signed up and paid, the travel agent hit him over the head with a bat, and threw him out the back door into the nearby river. Soon Dave entered the office, paid his hundred dollars and received the same treatment.

Some ten minutes later, the two rednecks awoke to find themselves floating down the river together.

"Gee," said Henry, "I wonder if they're serving any food on this cruise."

"I don't know," said Dave. "They didn't last year."

A poor farmer took his ailing wife to a doctor. The doctor examined her, put her through a barrage of tests, and then pulled the man aside.

"Your wife is very sick and I'm afraid she might not have long to live. I can try and cure her but it will be very expensive," the doctor explained. "Do you have any insurance?"

The distraught man looked at him. "No. But if you cure her, I'll pay you anything. Anything!"

"But I could treat her and she still might die," said the doctor shrewdly.

"Just treat her," the man pleaded. "Whether you cure her or kill her, I'll pay you whatever you ask even if I have to sell everything."

The doctor agreed, but despite his treatment, the woman passed away within the week. Remembering the conversation, the doctor presented a huge bill to the grieving farmer.

"Ten thousand!" the farmer gasped. "I can't possibly pay this. Can't we go to the judge in town and discuss some form of settlement?"

The doctor agreed. That afternoon the doctor, farmer, and judge sat down to discuss the fee. First the judge heard from the farmer. Then he turned to doctor. Well aware of the doctor's reputation for large fees, the judge asked, "Did you cure this man's wife?"

"Alas, no," replied the doctor, sadly shaking his head.

"Did you kill her?"

"Certainly not," protested the doctor.

"Well, under what terms of the agreement are you claiming a fee?"

Talley was caught speeding on the highway by a state trooper who was hiding behind a billboard.

As the trooper approached the car, he removed his sunglasses, smiled, and said, "Son, I've been waiting for you all morning."

"Well, officer," answered Talley, "I got here as fast as I could."

The two good ole boys were sitting at the bar having a couple of cold ones and discussing Southern women.

"I do believe that women in the South are the prettiest in the country," declared the first. The other man nodded in agreement. "And you know why? 'Cause they win all the beauty contests."

"And I think Southern women are the most polite," he went on, looking at his friend. "That's why they don't like group sex."

The other man looked at him quizzically. "They don't like group sex?"

"Nope. Too many thank you notes."

Clem was hired by an old farmer to help out during the harvest season. To make it easier for him to find his way to the field each day, the farmer suggested that Clem pick out a landmark to remember the tricky turnoff from the main road. Things went well the first two days on the job, but on his third trip, Clem got lost and arrived late.

"Didn't you pick out a landmark to help you remember where to turn?" asked the farmer.

"Sure did," replied Clem. "But the cows moved."

Terry and Gary were discussing their livestock at the local feed store.

"Had some problems with my herd," said Terry. "My prize bull was impotent. The vet came out and gave him some medicine, and now he seems okay."

The next week, the two farmers again met at the store.

"My bull's been having problems, too," said Gary. "What's the name of that medicine the vet prescribed?"

"Don't know," replied Bubba. "But it tastes like chocolate."

Jasper entered the local drugstore and asked for a can of talcum powder.

"Mennen's?" asked the clerk.

"Nope, Wimmen's," replied Jasper.

"Do you want it scented?" continued the clerk.

"Nope," answered Jasper. "I'll take it with me."

While walking through a strawberry patch on his farm, Roland was amazed to see a gigantic strawberry growing. This wasn't an ordinary, run-of-the-mill fruit, but an enormous record-setting specimen a good three-feet wide. Roland could not believe his eyes. He ran to a phone, called the Department of Agriculture, and was told that an agent would be sent out immediately to inspect the fruit.

A short time later, a car pulled up and a man in a suit stepped out. Roland brought him to the strawberry patch and showed him his incredible prize. The agent was dumbfounded.

"Do you think that strawberry is worth any money?" asked Roland.

"Probably," replied the government agent. "But it'll take me a while to figure out how much. I didn't expect anything quite so big."

After taking some measurements and examining the strawberry for a few minutes, the agent said, "This is going to take me a bit longer. Why don't you go back inside and I'll call you when I'm ready?"

Roland agreed and went back into the house. A short time later, he happened to look out the window and noticed the agent walking quickly back toward his car, with the fruit in his arms.

Roland flew out the door and called out to the agent, "Hey, what do you think you're doing there?"

Caught in the act, the agent turned toward Roland and explained, "Can't you guess? I came to seize your berry, not appraise it."

Stevie was out hunting when he came upon a beautiful young woman sunbathing in a clearing. Walking over, he said, "Pardon me, ma'am, but are you game?"

Looking the young man up and down, she replied, "Sure."

So he shot her.

"Next."

Q. How can you tell a redneck firing squad?

A. They stand in a circle.

Two young rednecks were walking down the highway, looking to hitch a ride. Eventually they were picked up by a huge grocery truck. The driver told them there was little room in front, but that they were welcome to ride in the back with his cargo. After a half hour or so, the truck, which had been traveling at a high rate of speed, swerved to avoid hitting an animal. The driver lost control, the truck ran onto the shoulder, and finally rolled over. Packages came tumbling down all around them, but the boys managed to make their way out relatively unscathed. Once in the light of day, they saw that the impact of the accident had been cushioned by the contents of the packages—assorted kinds of cheese.

"Wow," said one to the other. "What a friend we have in cheeses!"

A Texan, visiting Alabama, asked a local farmer how much acreage he had.

"Oh, I've got a big farm," said the redneck. "About one hundred and fifty acres."

"Shoot," replied the Texan, "back in Texas, when I get up in the morning, I get in my car, drive all day, and still can't get to the end of my property."

"I know what you mean," said the redneck. "I've got a car just like that."

Sally and Rita were vacationing in Florida when they happened to pass through Kissimmee. This prompted an argument about how the town's name was pronounced.

"KISS-imm-ee," said Sally.

"Kiss-IMM-ee," insisted Rita.

Convinced that she was right, Sally pulled her car into a local fast food restaurant and approached a man at the counter.

"Will you please tell my friend here how the name of this place is pronounced," asked Sally, "and since she's a little dense, please say it slowly."

"Sure," replied the man. "BUR-GER-KING."

Georgie was trudging down the road with his mule, when Brad drove up and offered him a ride into town. Georgie got into the truck, leaving the mule to run along behind. The mule kept up as Brad sped up to fifty miles per hour, and continued to keep pace as the truck sped up to seventy.

"I'm worried about your mule, Georgie," said Brad. "His tongue is hanging out of his mouth."

"Which side of his mouth?" asked Georgie.

"Left," replied Brad.

"Well, stay in this lane," said Georgie. "He's about to pass."

Q. How do you make a redneck girl's eyes sparkle?

A. Shine a flashlight in her ear.

A local preacher decided to sell his horse, and Annie was an interested buyer.

"I've got to warn you," said the preacher, "this animal only responds to 'church talk.' If you want him to go, say 'Praise the Lord', and if you want him to stop, say 'Hallelujah'."

A little disbelieving, Annie nonetheless mounted the horse and said, "Praise the Lord." The horse took off at a trot. "Praise the Lord," repeated Annie, and the horse picked up the pace. One more "Praise the Lord," and the horse began to race along at a full gallop. Suddenly, Annie caught sight of a cliff dead ahead. Frantically she screamed, "Hallelujah," and the horse came to a stop a scant foot from the edge.

A relieved Annie wiped the sweat from her brow with her handkerchief. "Praise the Lord!" she said.


Josh was explaining to his boss why he was late for work that cold winter morning.

"It was so slippery out," he said, "every time I took a step forward, I slipped back two."

"Oh, yeah?" said his boss eyeing him suspiciously. "Then how did you manage to make it here?"

"I finally gave up," said Josh, "and started back home."


Bumper sticker in North Carolina: "Support cats: run over a chicken."

Frankie Lee and Andy were out walking when they came upon a well in the ground.

"How deep do you think it is?" asked Frankie Lee.

"I don't know," replied Andy. "Let's drop a rock in it and wait for it to hit bottom."

The two rednecks did so, but heard no sound. They found a larger rock and threw it in, but still no noise. A short distance away, they saw a large log. They each took an end and managed to toss it into the well, but still nothing. While they were waiting to hear the splash, a goat ran right between them and jumped into the hole.

As they stood there wondering what happened, Billie Bob came up to them and asked, "Hey, have you fellas seen a goat?"

"Well, as a matter of fact we have," said Frankie Lee. "A goat just ran by us and jumped into that hole."

"Oh, that couldn't have been my goat," said Billie Bob. "Mine was tied up to a log."


A large group of men gathered in an Atlanta bar were being amused by a fellow who claimed to have the uncanny skill of identifying each man's nationality by the shape of his head.

"That's a lotta bull," yelled out a redneck in the group.

"Oh, yeah?" said the man. "Well, not only can I tell a man's nationality, I can even tell what school he attended. For example, this gentleman over here went to Princeton. Am I right, sir?"

"Why, yes, you are," replied the fellow.

"I could tell by the cut of your clothes," explained the man. "Now, this man here, he's from Tulane. Isn't that right?"

"Yes, it is."

"I was able to tell by his manner of speech. And this man here is from the University of Virginia. I can tell by the crest on his blazer."

Turning to the redneck, he said in a loud voice:

"And you, my friend, are from the University of Alabama. Am I right?"

The redneck was flabbergasted.

"Well, I'll be. How could you tell?" he stammered.

"Easy," replied the man. "I noticed the insignia on your class ring a few moments ago when you reached up to pick your nose."

Lucius and his fiancée, Bobbie Jo, went to the town hall to apply for a marriage license. After filling out the papers, the clerk told them, "This license is good for thirty days."

"Gosh," said Lucius. "Don't you have one that's 'till death do us part'?"

Brothers Jared and John went to an employment agency looking for work. Jared was called first for an interview.

"It says here you're a pilot," said the counselor. "That's great. There's always a need for pilots. I have a job available for you right here."

Jared left and John entered the room.

"And what do you do?" asked the counselor.

"Ahm a tree cutter," replied John.

"I'm sorry," said the counselor. "There are no job openings for tree cutters."

"That's ridiculous," screamed John. "How come you got a job for my brother, but nothing for me?"

"Well," explained the counselor, "your brother is a pilot. That's a specialized skill."

"What do you mean specialized?" asked John. "I cut the wood and he piles it!"


Two visiting business executives were having a drink at a small country bar. As the bartender served them, he heard a beep beep sound coming from inside the jacket of one of the men. As the bartender watched, the executive took a pen out of his jacket, and started talking into it. When he finished, he noticed the puzzled looks on the faces of the bartender and the other customers.

"Oh," he explained, "I was just answering a call on my state-of-the-art cellular pen."

A little while later, another beep sounded. The second executive took off his hat and started talking into it. When he finished, he put his hat back on and explained, "That was a call on my state-of-the-art cellular hat."

A few minutes later, a redneck at the end of the bar let loose with a loud burp.

"Quick," he yelled. "Get me a piece of paper. I got a fax comin' in!"